Pick It, Thrift It & Flip It

A comprehensive Guide To Making Money Picking, Thrifting & Flipping Items At Garage Sales, Auctions & Thrift Stores

Introduction

Thrifting is exciting in itself but reselling thrifted merchandise and products, now that is both exciting and lucrative for you. The reselling industry has grown exponentially over the past few years. The demand is there, from people who are now more cost conscious of their resources, collectors willing to pay good money and from other avid thrifters. The supply is also there, from chain, independent and other specialty thrift stores. The only thing missing is you!

This book gives you a step by step guide on how to start your reselling business. It will tell you everything about the types of thrift stores, the best thrifted products to resell, the locations of the stores and even both the advantages and challenges of the reselling business.

It will also tell you how to prepare for your reselling business, the tools, materials and requirements you need, the way to assess and inspect thrifted products before you purchase and even a list of items that are prohibited for reselling.

Business management tools such as inventory management, bookkeeping and networking and promotions are also included. Bonus sections giving you a quick action guide, checklist, thrifting lingo and sample products are also found in this book.

To maximize the ebook format, links to videos are included. Instead of only reading how to assess products and what kind of thrifted merchandise are being sold today, these videos will easily get the message across.

Begin thrifting today and tomorrow, start reselling!

Table of Contents

Step One: Discover Thrifting

Types & Differences of Thrift Stores

There may just be as many thrift stores as there are thrifters. Each thrifter will have his own specific interest, preference or need. To satisfy this economic demand, thrift stores provide a wide variety supply. Before talking about the merchandises that are sold in thrift stores, it is important to differentiate the actual thrift stores that sell them.

This is important because certain types of stores have more inventories making a trip to one of them very time efficient. However, these large stores will have a variety of products to sell and you may not find the specific item you are looking for. On the other hand, some thrift stores are small and out of the way making the trip potentially time consuming. However, these small and specialty stores have unique merchandise that may not be available anywhere else.

There are generally five kinds of thrift stores: chain, independent, vintage, specialty and consignment thrift stores. Chain thrift stores are those that are run and owned by large companies. Since these stores are usually large and occupy prime locations in town, to cover overhead expenses such as salaries, rent and other costs, they are usually priced high. However, they offer huge selections and visiting one can already fill your inventory. Remember, when a thrift store is located in suburban areas that are upscale, expect new items but sold at high prices. At the same time, these stores have huge customer traffic and it is easy to miss out on deals when you are not there on time. If you plan to sell primarily usable and new items, such as overruns that are sold cheap, chain stores are the place to go.

Independent thrift stores are usually owned by a family or a group of friends that share the same interests. While they have few selections and may be located in more difficult to reach areas, the price and quality of the selections may more than make up for the trip. This store also has small turnover rates, meaning they do not regular replace their stocks with new ones. Since each proprietor basically controls the entire business, expect one store to be very different from another. One thrift store may have good standards, such as customer service, openness to negotiation or care for products and another store may have the exact opposite. Patience is required for this type of stores since these stores are the best place to find the best deals.

Vintage stores exist in a plane just below chain but above independent stores. This store is proud of selling antiques and vintage items only, however they will have their own criteria of what qualifies an item to be called an antique or vintage. Take note, technically, an item must be proven to be at least 25 years old to be considered an antique. Most of these stores may consider an antique to be anything that looks old. Also this store may also be in the same business as you. This means they need to cover both the purchase and cost of reselling on their sale prices, making the price more expensive. However, this store has its unique advantage. You can request the owner to be on the lookout for your specific requirements and products that come in a set are more complete in this store.

Specialty stores are one of the best types of stores in the industry. Although they may only cater to specific niches, you are guaranteed that whatever is found on this store has good quality and provenance. This is a haven for you if you plan to sell a specific type of product. If you want to make your inventory diverse with quality products, you can go to this store. You can shop on this store to fill the specific niche in your inventory. Take note that prices in this store are higher than their more humble counterparts.

Consignment stores are not technically thrift stores because they are only third party resellers. This store does not really own their merchandise but only sell them for a commission. Quality and prices are high. The advantage of this store is that the store is usually highly organized.

Another store that is not technically a thrift store but is usually discussed along with genuine thrift stores are pawn shops. Just by their nature, they do not actually sell cheap items; in fact they sell high end items such as jewelry, musical instruments, electronics, watches and other high priced items. Do not expect to spend a little amount of money to purchase anything here. You can however bargain as with other thrift stores. If your thrift shop is about selling to customers with stronger purchasing powers, pawn shops are the place to go.

Merchandise & Products

Virtually anything can be sold in thrift stores. However, remember you are shopping at these stores not for personal use but for personal profit through reselling. Instead of discussing each of the many items that are sold, it is much better to talk about the items that you can buy.

Here are the top 20 items that you should buy not only because they are sold cheap but also because they have the highest potential for profit:

1. Books
2. Discontinued board and video games
3. Vintage Pyrex
4. Old mugs
5. Vintage glassware
6. Art frames
7. Sterling silver
8. Dinnerware
9. Ceramics with embossed stamps
10. Jackets
11. Branded clothes
12. Vintage Desk lamps
13. Vintage Barware
14. Colored glassware with patterns
15. Cobalt blue and Perfect mason bottles

16. Crystals

17. Vintage globes

18. Vintage quilts

19. Branded or vintage fashion accessories

20. Discontinued stuffed toys

There will certainly be more things other than those in the list above that you can watch out for in a thrift shop. The list above is by no means exhaustive; it only shows you the most lucrative items that you can consider for your business. At the end of the day, the decision relies on you on which items you would want your reselling business to have. This can be based not only on your desire for profit but also for your passion for the business. Remember, half of the fun of the business should come from profit and the other half should come from your sheer enjoyment of your endeavor.

Here is another list, this time of items that you may consider not purchasing.

1. Appliances used to process raw food stuffs

2. Undergarments

3. Bathing suits

4. Mattresses

5. Cosmetics

6. Pillows

7. Helmets

8. Old blenders

9. Wigs

10. Used linen

11. Incomplete games

12. Mass produced artworks

Some of the reasons why you should not even buy them aside from the safety and hygiene concerns are that they are simply not in demand. Board games are extremely lucrative, only if you have the complete set. A buyer will hesitate in buying an incomplete board game even if he is a collector. So there is a risk that you will not get a return on your investment. These items also represent a very narrow profit margin; this means that you might still be able to resell them. However, the profit you get from it might not cover the cost of buying, transporting, storing and selling them in the first place.

Locating Thrift Stores & Thrifting Tips

Finding the best thrift store is necessary for you, this is your first step to satisfy the sourcing needs of your business. You can plan out a sourcing day where you will visit several thrift stores that can make up your first batch of your inventory.

With technology, internet and search engines, finding the thrift store that is nearest or most accessible to you becomes easier. Plus, not only can you find the actual location, you can make a plan to visit a variety of thrift stores. Aside from that, you can shortlist thrift stores that you think may be worthwhile to visit based on their profile or information made available over the Internet.

Aside from your favorite search engines, here are some links that you can use to locate your thrift store:

1. Thrift store directory

2. Thrift store listing

3. <u>Thrift shop finder</u>

4. <u>Sample Google map search for thrift stores</u>

5. <u>Online thrift store directory</u>

Of course, finding a thrift store is only one half of the search. The next step is that you should learn to be a savvy thrift store buyer when you are actually in the thrift store itself. Finding a thrift store is one thing but shopping well is another. Here are some tips to help you make the best visit in a thrift store:

1. Before even locating your store, you need to define your niche. This can be determined by your business goals, the current trends in the thrifting industry such as fads and best sellers and plain passion for the business. Remember aside from money, you need to carry with you a certain level of knowledge when you are out shopping. The more information you have on an item you are looking for, the better the chances you can find it. Conduct some research prior to making your first purchase.

2. Next, have a limit on your resources; this is not just about a limitation on your budget but also on your time and health. Set a limit on how much you will spend in a day. Divide that amount into a limit on how much you will spend on a store, especially if you are planning to make a thrift store tour. If you can set another limit on how much you will spend per item, then that would even be better. The more financial controls you have the better the chances of you widening your profit margins. Do the same for your time, how many hours in the day for the entire tour, hours per store and time deciding on an item. Be careful about your health too, thrift stores are notorious for dust, mildew and other allergens that can affect your health.

3. Next consider scheduling your thrifting during low customer traffic, mornings and afternoons of weekdays are the best time to go. Consider also the schedule of the thrift shop, when does it have new items where you can get first pick of the merchandise? When does it go on sale? When is the store owner present so you can immediately get a decision for a request for discount? Most thrift stores have special promos to entice customers, such as discounts on special days in the calendar, 50% off on anything made of plastic or anything made of ceramic and other gimmicks.

4. Now that you have the budget, the time and best schedule to visit the thrift store, it is now time to enter. Regardless of the type or size of the store, devote time on one area at a time. Instead of moving around haphazardly, make efficient use of your time by slowly but methodically search at each section. The best items are usually nearest the counter so the cashier can look out after them and in the middle aisles to get the most traffic.

5. Only few types of thrift stores have fixed prices and even those with price tags can offer discounts when you ask them. Haggling or bargaining is one of the most important skills you need in the thrifting business. It may mean only a few dollars of savings but those few dollars will eventually add up. Remember, negotiating can bring the price down to such a level when you can reach your target profit margin. Negotiation is a broad topic and involves several techniques and strategies. Some of them include opening at a price that is half of the original selling price, offering to buy more if a discount is given on the total price and suggesting that you will bring your business elsewhere.

6. Remember a bit of courtesy can go a long way. Build a working relationship with the sellers and proprietors. With this relationship, you may have access to certain perks that few other customers may have. For example,

you can have advanced notice of certain sales and schedules, access to inventory before they are displayed or reserve an item for you while you are thinking about the purchase.

7. Most thrifters suggest that you free yourself from the pressure of having to buy something every time you go to a store. It is perfectly acceptable that you go to a store and leave empty handed. With this relief from pressure, you do not have to make forced or hasty decision that your business does not really require.

8. Do not be afraid to go out of your comfort zone in your usual thrift stores. Most experienced thrifters thrive on the opportunity to explore new stores on new places. Constantly find opportunities for you to thrift shop anywhere you go. For example, if you are out of town or on a long vacation, try visiting a thrift store in that location. Since no two thrift stores are exactly alike, you may surprise yourself with the merchandise available or a new business relationship that you can build.

9. It is also important to check the policy for returns in the thrift store. This is especially needed if you are in a new and unfamiliar store. You also need this information when you are purchasing items that are notorious for their potential for being unusable after you purchase them. For example, electronics may seem to work while testing them at the store only to find out when you go home that it broke again. Each store will have their specific set of policies on specific items in their merchandise.

10. One of the key elements for thrift shopping success is frequency. The more stores you visit the more merchandise you can find. This is also important to create the exposure and experience beginner thrifters need.

11. With the Internet, most thrift stores, especially the bigger ones, will have their own website. For the more independently owned stores, they will at least have an online presence in a blog or social media account. Ask them to include you in their mailing list. This will keep you in the loop wherever you are. Notices of sale, discounts or new batch of inventory can be received as soon as they are ready.

12. Lastly and a tip that may be outside your control is plain luck. Know that the thrifting business primarily relies on your skills as a business owner and as a thrifter. However, a portion of the business still relies on luck. You may uncover from a pile of cheap items could be an overlooked designer bag, a discontinued board game may just be in a corner shelf that few people browse or an authentic but unidentified antique could be in plain sight.

Pros & Cons of Reselling

The reselling business may be a lucrative business. It has many advantages but it is by no means a perfect business. It will also have its disadvantages. However, instead of looking them in a negative way, look at them as challenges that you can anticipate. When you know these constraints in advance, you can better prepare for them.

Pros

Demand

There is a huge demand for thrifted products coming from three major sources: the economic crisis that made buyers more budget conscious, the collectors in search of the item that can satisfy their hobbies and the trend and popularity of thrifted products. This means that there will always be customers in your reselling business. However, it will be up to you maintain your relationship with your customers to make them come back for you.

Passion

If you happen to have the passion for the thrifting and reselling business then this is the ideal business environment for you. This is because you can get to live out your passion while earning money at the same time. Most resellers started as dedicated thrifters and the reselling business is a natural step to the next level. Aside from using the profit for other expenses or investing back to the business, you can use it for your personal thrifting.

Margin

Depending on your choice of inventory , your ability to sell and effective business processes and of course, sheer luck of finding a valuable item, the reselling business can truly be lucrative. Doubling the investment represents the lowest profit margin in the business, this means that you can triple, quadruple and multiply your profit to even greater percentages.

Training

Since the thrifting business requires a relatively smaller investment and less risk compared to other business start ups, this business can be a safe training ground for you. This will provide you with hands-on training on business processes such as sourcing, selling, negotiation, budgeting, customer service and other business related process. Later on, you can apply these same skills to future endeavors.

Cons

Growing pains

Starting a thrifting business is hard but once you set up and open store, you may expect that customers will come flocking to your store. Expect people to visit only out of curiosity on the newest opened store in town. Few or maybe no one may even purchase an item at all in the first day. You need to make yourself known, prove your credibility and create a loyal customer base before you can reach the success of your thrifting business. For some, it may take a short or long time but with sound business decisions, you will get there.

Competition

Of course with all the benefits and relatively few challenges of the reselling business, there are already people out there who are considering the same business. Some may already have started. This means that aside from the well known thrifting stores, there are also competitions from people who are opening their businesses like you. However with the right business skills, you can make yourself and your reselling business stand out among the rest.

Step Two: Prepare for the Business

Tools, Materials & Requirements

Now that you have inventory the next thing you need to do is sell. There are two ways that you can prepare for the first days of the business and the choice is dependent on the kind of store that you want. You can either open a traditional brick and mortar thrift store or an online thrift store.

Both types require these things:

1. Business plan, this will help you determine everything from the merchandise you need to look for and resell, the target customers you are preparing the business for, the promotions and networking activities you need, type of store and other business concerns.

2. Pricing scheme, this will give you the range of the price you need to buy an item from a thrift shop to the amount you will resell it. You also need to make a tolerable allowance for negotiation.

3. Shopping supplies, this is your thrift store shopping kit; this can include tape measurement for clothes, measuring tape for furniture, disposable gloves and masks for handling merchandise and other personal items.

4. Adequate inventory, your inventory must be complete and satisfy the demands of your buyers. Aside from the quality and quantity, you also need to make replenishing your inventory as efficient as possible.

5. Cleaning supplies, everything from simple cleaning materials such as soaps, wipes and dusters to the heavy duty items such as disinfectants, polishers and other specialized tools are needed depending on your inventory.

6. Packing supplies, if you plan to ship your items, you will need bubble wraps, boxes, packaging tape and a partner courier.

7. Storage space, you need enough space to house your items while you are waiting for the in store items to sell. You need plastic or textile sheets to cover them, shelves or cabinets to organize them for easy location, access and security.

8. Mobile apps, you need to take advantage of the developments in technology to increase efficiency and therefore the performance of your business. This goes beyond simple Excel files of your inventory or an email account for your communication. Consider installing mobile apps on your smartphone to keep yourself updated and in the loop wherever you go. For example, download apps of the popular thrift stores platform like eBay and Etsy. You can browse them anywhere you go. A recent development in the productivity app industry is the IFTTT. This is a very nifty tool that can automate simple tasks that will give you the extra minute you need for more important tasks. For example, you can set IFTTT to automatically notify you via text message that a specific item you are looking for in eBay has just been posted.

Brick and mortar stores require these:

1. License to resell, visit your town hall for this permit

2. Tax ID number, again visit your local government office

3. Insurance, consult your broker for this protection

4. Location, ask your real estate agent or the listings

5. Perfect balance of location and rent, the better the location, the higher the rent

6. Sketch or a floor plan of how to arrange your merchandise and store fixtures.

7. Parking for your customers and area to receive your shipment, especially for large sized merchandise such as furniture

8. Shelves, cabinets and other tools to display your merchandise. Clothes need hanger, racks and sometime mannequins. Plates need display stands. Electronics need to have testers.

9. Personnel, such as a cashier or a salesperson, unless you plan to handle the store yourself.

Online stores require these:

1. A functional computer and dependable connection.

2. An online platform that is friendly for resellers.

3. An established logistical system that involves storing, retrieving and shipping merchandise once sold.

Purchasing Criteria

Remember, this is a business and you have to always be aware of your return of investment or ROI. Here is a simple number to help you gauge how much you need to buy an item so you can sell it at a desired profit: 50%. Most experienced resellers recommend that for you to cover not only the actual purchase price of the item but also the cost of selling it, such as gas, rent, storage and other overhead or recurring expenses, you need the 50% rule.

Basically the rule says that you need to know the current market rate of the item in retail. For example, you find a pair of jeans that costs $220 in a brand new condition in a retail store. Now you need to take into consideration your target customers, one of the reasons that they will buy thrifted products is because they are cheap. Chances are they will also know that the jeans they want also cost $220 in the mall. They will only buy a thrifted version of the jeans if it costs at least half, which is around $110. With that target selling price, next you need to set your profit margin. If you want a 50% profit margin you need to buy the jeans for at least $50.

Take note that this is a rule when your target customer is someone who is on a tight budget or weak purchasing power. The thrifting business becomes more lucrative when you are able to tap the strong purchasing powers of individuals who are willing to spend more on an item because of their rarity, quality, collectability, personal attachment and other factors. If this is your customer base, then the 50% rule can be modified.

In this case, you need to research an item very well. Consider looking for similar items online; find out their average prices and bidding amounts. Consult an expert if needed so you can get a professional and objective appraisal of the real value of your item. Adjust your pricing accordingly.

Quality Control

Each thrifted product will have its own criteria to determine its quality or authenticity; these are needed to help you decide on the purchase. Here are some tips to control the quality of your inventory by purchasing only assessed merchandise:

1. For vintage glassware, look for embossed stamps at the bottom. If they are only printed on the surface, chances are they are fakes. Look for chips and other signs of damage. Lightly touch the surface of the glassware and feel for sign of roughness, especially in the rims. If you encounter any bumps, they may be damages unseen to the naked eye.

2. For designer merchandise, like bags, wallets and other fashion accessories, pay close attention to the quality of the material. Genuine leather is rough to the touch with very small indentations but it is very flexible and bendable. The color will have darkened called patina.

Check for serial numbers. Hardware, such as clasps, zippers and other metals in the item will have the logo of the designer. Of course, Made in China is a telltale sign that it is a fake. Each designer will have his own set of distinguishing characteristics and the corresponding ways to discern a genuine from an imitation. Do appropriate research when you plan to fill your inventory with these designer items.

3. For clothing, a good standard you can use is if you would not wear the item, it probably will not sell too. Check for stains, spots, tears or missing buttons. Color should still be as vibrant as possible, faded items may not sell. Reverse the clothes so you can also inspect their inner sides, linings and other parts that may not be readily noticeable. While some of these damages can be easily repaired, it may reduce the price when the buyers see signs of repair or replaced buttons.

4. For board games and similar items, make sure that all the pieces are intact. One sure way to know if it is complete is to find the manual; it should have a list of all the contents of the game.

5. For electronics, make sure to test them if they work. If the seller refuses, then it might a sign that it is not working. If the seller claims that it is broken but can be repaired easily, consult with an electrician. Check also for completeness. If there are missing parts, ask your electrician if the part can be replaced.

6. For antiques, ask for provenance. This is any kind of evidence that proves that the antique is as old as the seller claims it to be. For example, it can be an old family picture dated more than 25 years ago but the picture has the item in the background.

7. For new items, such as overruns, check for barcodes, tags and other information that is provided by manufacturers. These are important to give you more

information that you can use to help you decide to make the purchase or how much to resell it.

Here are tutorial videos on how to check for the quality of thrifted merchandise.

1. Clothes
    https://www.youtube.com/watch?v=PdVgusoOxXM

2. Glassware
    https://www.youtube.com/watch?v=GiiL26qH5BY

3. Designer Bags
    https://www.youtube.com/watch?v=ZEV7_vpOM64

4. Jewelry
    https://www.youtube.com/watch?v=aTLJToIerWU

5. Electronics
    https://www.youtube.com/watch?v=Dl6XjyyDuRI

6. Crystals
    https://www.youtube.com/watch?v=T3C4OoYzxd8

7. Antiques
    https://www.youtube.com/watch?v=YtJTdwT8MR0

8. Silverware
    https://www.youtube.com/watch?v=l23h_TPKBNg

Prohibited Items

As wide as the selection of products that you can buy in thrift stores and resell in your business, there are also items that are regulated and prohibited. It is important that you are aware of these products that cannot be sold as you will break the law. A recent study made the US Consumer Product Safety Commission published the results of their research. These products were banned by the Commission because of their hazardous nature that poses a risk for to consumer health and life and their failure to meet the safety standards of the Commission.

The top three items that were banned are:

1. Clothing drawstrings. These are found in children's clothes that when worn out has the potential of strangulating a child when caught on cribs, doors or equipment in the playground.

2. Hair dryers. When sold second hand, these appliances may have already lost the rubber wiring that can protect owners from electrocution. Sometimes, a hair dryer will still have the rubber wiring intact but the plug may be wrong kind. Hair dryers are supposed to have a rectangular shaped plug but some dryers will not have this feature.

3. Cribs. These items also present a risk to children because they may not meet the prescribed safety standards. Some of the violations include cribs that do not have adequate sizes, exposed metal knobs, and chipped paints and catch points that can potentially strangle a baby.

Other items that were banned are:

1. Halogen floor lamps

2. Playpens

3. Car seat carriers

4. Toy basketball nets

5. Child safety gates

6. Bunk beds

7. Infant swings

8. Cedar chests

9. Bean bag chairs

10. Lawn darts

Best Store Locations

Brick and mortar stores

1. Traffic. Choose a location that has high traffic from customers or from passing cars. This makes sure that your store is highly visible. Try to find a store space as close to the intersection as possible since you can get the most visibility in this area.

2. Other thrift stores. Instead of moving away from them, it is better to open your store as close to them as possible. This is necessary when you are just starting your reselling business. Most thrifters, who regularly visit the established thrift stores, will take every opportunity to shop on another.

3. Windows. Consider a store that already has large display windows so you show off your merchandise to even those who are outside. You can also save a lot of money from having to improve the store to suit your needs. Adequate parking and storage space, presence of security and surveillance and other amenities make an ideal store.

4. Rent and expenses. Check your income streams and anticipated profit. Aside from rent, the store space must be ready for your occupancy. Check for signs of disrepair or improvements that you have to make. These expenses may be charged to you and not your landlord. Also, check for leasing terms; try to close a deal on a short term contract such as 6 months so you can test out your business before you commit long term.

5. As much as possible, try to open your store near a community of rich individuals or families. They have strong purchasing powers, they may not buy the second hand clothes or used furniture in your store but they are definitely in the market for antiques, collectibles and authentic designer accessories.

Online stores

1. Ebay. This online platform is arguably the best place to open your reselling business. The interface is user friendly, the starter seller accounts are free and its customer base is large and its reach is wide. No other online platform can compare to Ebay in terms of the reselling business.

2. Etsy. This platform is gaining popularity as an alternative to Ebay. Consider this a combination of specialty and vintage thrift store. If your inventory belongs to this category, Etsy is another option for you.

3. Social media. Facebook, Pinterest, Instagram and other social media that can host both text and pictures can also be a place where you can set up your virtual store. They are free, have huge traffic and easy to use. However, their true potential lies on their ability to promote your business.

4. Blog. Instead of relying on these platforms that can limit the way you sell your merchandise, such as prescribed rules for posting an ad, with a blog you have almost total control of the content. Design a theme, customize a link and other features are made available when you have a blog to your own.

5. Combination. The best reseller will not choose just one of these platforms but choose a combination of them, thereby doubling or tripling your reach to customers. A multi-platform reselling business will not incur additional costs just a few minutes of registration and uploading of your merchandise.

Most resellers recommend that if you are a beginner reseller, you may opt to start with an online store first. It is a safe investment that incurs minimal to almost no cost. You can use it as a training ground and as means of generating enough capital to invest and upgrade to a traditional brick and mortar store.

Step Three: Manage the Business

Organization & Business Processes

It will be easy to lose track of your merchandise without the appropriate inventory management tools. You can use something as simple as a log book of ins and outs of merchandise or more sophisticated software that can record purchase price, date of purchase, location in the storage and other information. The lesson here is not which inventory tool you choose but that you need an inventory in the first place. You may be able to handle less than 10 items but when your inventory grows and sale peaks, you may run the risk of misplacing or mis-pricing your merchandise.

Online stores will do the bookkeeping of your income and revenues but for the rest of the monitoring of your finances it will be up to you. You need to be as meticulous with this as possible as may be potential tax implications. To be safe have an accountant that can do the books for you on a monthly basis. On the other hand, instead of this additional cost, you can download any free accounting software. They are usually easy to use and generate several financial reports that can help you make sound financial decisions.

Cash is usually the mode of payment for thrift stores. However, most buyers these days rely on credit and debit cards for purchases. Make sure that you have both options available for them. Resellers discourage accepting checks, especially for high value items.

Ideally, you should be able to handle the business yourself. However, if you do not have the time, it is best to hire your staff. You need at least one cashier, who can handle the payments and the inventory. At least one another person, this time in charge of selling and moving of merchandise is also required.

Consider opening an account to your local courier. This will provide you with more efficient shipping and handling of thrifted products you bought or merchandise that you were able to sell.

Do's & Don'ts

Do's

Love it. Regardless of the thrift products you choose, the profits you make or the locations you sell, the reselling business requires you to actually love the business. Thrifting will definitely be a lot of work, rummaging through boxes, visiting auctions and endless bargaining with sellers. Only if you truly feel passionate about the thrifting business will all these activities become not only easy but also fun to do.

Know the brands. This is especially needed for those who plan to include clothes and fashion accessories in their business. Thrift stores are filled with clothes and you may find yourself paralyzed from so many options. Knowing the brands will have help you shortlist your choices into a few but profitable numbers. Plus, since thrift stores buy in bulk they may never know what is on their inventory at all. You may be able to spot a designer dress that was overlooked by the store owner.

Be thrifty. This may seem like common sense but most reseller seem to overspend. This is because some of these products might be very cheap to you that you will not mind paying for them at full price. You may think that a couple of dollars more that you are asked to pay will not make a difference. Remember, the lower the purchase price, the higher the profit margin. To get the lowest purchase price possible, you need the next "do."

Practice negotiation. This skill can benefit almost all aspects of your business. From lowering the purchase price, bargaining for shipping time and cost, getting a great deal in rent, storage fees and other recurring expenses and to the final sale with your customers. There is a stereotype that women are better making a bargain than men. Women are said to be able to smooth or charm their way in a negotiation while men are impatient to finalize the purchase. Whether this is true or not, the fact is as a business owner you need to develop or refine this skill.

Don'ts

Overstock. Most resellers recommend that you keep just enough inventories to fill your store and a few on the storage available in the store itself. This is because when you overstock, you may incur additional costs such as storage and maintenance expenses. There is also a chance that the items held in stock may only get damaged or dirty, prompting more expenses. Try to keep your supply chain management as efficient as possible.

Ignore hygiene and protection. When you go to source your products or when you handle your recent purchases, remember to wear adequate protection. Disposable gloves and masks are needed when you enter musty stores or hold objects that are dirty. Be especially careful if you are sensitive to allergens. If you are handling thrifted items such as furniture, sharp kitchenware or other hazardous items, use more protective clothing.

Rely solely on your skills. Have a pool of experts. By the very nature of thrift products, you will encounter second hand, broken but repairable, damaged but restorable and unknown but identifiable products. Most electronic products require only a few changes on their parts for them to work again. A quick repaint or application of varnish can restore an antique to its glory. Products that you find with doubtful provenance or unknown origins can be authenticated by experts.

Start big. Scale your expenses, operations and other business activities based on the performance of your business. Novice resellers may fail on their business when they invest too much on overhead and other miscellaneous expenses. When this happens, they may have good profit margins but as a result of starting big, the profits will not enough to cover the expenses.

Promotions & Networking

As good as your inventory is, as competitive as your prices are or as perfect as your location is, your customers will not reach you when you do not promote your business. You may get some traffic from passersby who chances upon your store. However, you cannot be sure that they will purchase anything. You need to promote your store to be able to make your business known to the right people using the right tools.

Although traditional promotions can work, such as advertising on a local paper or posting flyers around the town, this usually costs a certain amount of money. Especially for beginner resellers, advertising expenses may be the least of your concerns. As much as possible, your investment must all be geared toward expenses that will have a direct yield on your business efforts, such as inventory.

The best advertisement platforms that you can use and that are also free are the variety of social media. You can register your store as a business in Facebook; create an Instagram account where you can post pictures of your items or Tweet links of your Ebay and other social media profile. For a minimal cost, you can also pay Facebook to show your business account on the news feeds of your targeted users.

Expert resellers recommend that advertising expenses must not be found in any budget of beginner sellers. These kinds of costs are meant to be spent only for more established resellers who have the funds to cover the expenses. Instead, you may opt to begin with these free but still effective means of promoting your product.

Networking is also important. Be a part of a community of thrifters and resellers. You can gain a lot of insights and tricks of the trade from them. They can point you out to their usual spots for thrifting that may not be popularly known. Without being a competition to them, they can give you sources for your specific inventory needs. Aside from this community, you also need a network of professionals or experts. These are your resource persons who can provide expert advice and service, such as appraisal, restoration, repair and other skills that you may not have.

Appendix 1: Quick Action Guide & Checklist

Here is a rudimentary quick action guide and checklist of everything you need to know about setting up your business for reselling thrifted merchandise. It follows the basic step by step guide of a business development plan.

Action 1: Identify Your Niche

Checklist:

- o Passion
- o Interest
- o Currently existing inventory, if applicable

Action 2: Research the Price, Trends & Demands

Checklist:

- o Web research for prices, use Ebay to search for items
- o Desired profit; refer to 50% rule

Action 3: Source Your Products

Checklist:

- o Investment money or capital
- o Location of thrift stores, refer to locating thrift stores
- o Shopping at thrift stores, refer to thrift store shopping

- List of thrifted items to look for, refer to merchandise and products

- List of thrifted items to avoid, refer to merchandise and products

- Assessment of merchandise, refer to quality control

- Network of experts and logistics partners, such as appraisers, electricians and shippers

Action 4: Start the business

Checklist:

- Thrifting kit, refer to tools, materials and requirements

- Business location, refer to best locations to resell

- Business operations, refer to organization and business processes and do's and don'ts

- Strategic partnerships, refer to promotions and networking

Appendix 2: Thrifting Lingo

If you are a beginner in the thrifting business it might get confusing for you when you here the lingo used by experienced thrifters. To avoid confusion and also to make yourself part of the community, it is best to learn the meanings behind these jargon. Use them on your thrifting tour and gain the respect of your peers.

GDUB or The GW: This refers to Goodwill, the national chain of thrift stores. This is a chain that is meant to provide funding for social services.

SALVO, SAL VAL or the S&A: This refers to the Salvation Army, another chain of thrift stores that receives and then resells donated items to fund its services for the poor.

FLEA'IN: Basically means going to the flea market.

CO-SIGN: This refers to consignment stores or consigned goods.

YARD SAILING: This refers to going to a series garage or yard sales.

ESTATE HUNT: This refers to going to estate auctions or sales. When you are on the hunt you are planning to buy a specific item on the sale.

TAG SALES: Another term related to estate hunts but this time refers to a price set by a middleman to sell items in the estate sale.

SECOND HAND: An item that was previously owned.

THRIFT TOUR: A day dedicated to visits to various thrift stores.

SECOND MACYS: A thrift store that has a large selection of merchandise, similar to the department store of its name.

THRIFT BUST: Leaving a thrift store empty handed.

THRIFT MISS: This refers to your feeling that there is a possibility that you can find an item you are looking for or not.

STOCKPILE SAVER: Purposely purchasing items that your business may not yet need but you anticipate future profits for it.

THRIFTING AFFAIR: A special relationship you develop with the proprietor, employees and the thrift store itself.

THRIFTING CHEAT: When you break your loyalty to your thrifting affair by visiting another thrift store.

FIND: This refers to a purchase of an item that is really good or very profitable.

DEADSTOCK: A merchandise of the store that remained in the warehouse or storage.

THRIFT TOOLS: This refers to your set of materials, supplies and other items that are needed for your business or tools that can help make the visit to thrift stores more enjoyable and efficient.

SALVAGE SALE: This refers to the event when consigned merchandise is left unsold and the seller will reduce prices just to break even.

THRIFT CRUNCH: Visiting a store for less than 20 minutes.

THRIFT HOG: A rude thrifter.

THRIFT SISTER: Your regular companion during shopping.

Appendix 3: 20 Sample Thrifted Products

1. Books
   https://www.youtube.com/watch?v=_6hcGCagSMI

2. Toys
   https://www.youtube.com/watch?v=pgWN1hropLo

3. Pyrex
   https://www.youtube.com/watch?v=fU3ULL_jgik

4. Video games
   https://www.youtube.com/watch?v=PUG69cOiTws

5. Glassware
   https://www.youtube.com/watch?v=yZIOpu692zM

6. Art https://www.youtube.com/watch?v=tD5yxTW9yro

7. Silver
   https://www.youtube.com/watch?v=wx3H4rfi8ks

8. Dinnerware
   https://www.youtube.com/watch?v=3NXtseJklHI

9. Ceramics
   https://www.youtube.com/watch?v=lpIo2_wbJEg

10. Branded clothing
    https://www.youtube.com/watch?v=MKdmHMo1FZM

11. Jackets
    https://www.youtube.com/watch?v=28oYv8iKbls

12. Vintage barware
    https://www.youtube.com/watch?v=uNmojnPwd1E

13. Crystals
https://www.youtube.com/watch?v=bRtiJC0M7wg

14. Electronics
https://www.youtube.com/watch?v=XjNmsi22LA8

15. Designer accessories
https://www.youtube.com/watch?v=k7ULxkL8ibQ

16. Stuffed toys
https://www.youtube.com/watch?v=iNJM8JFY8p8

17. Antiques
https://www.youtube.com/watch?v=rUPOomwpapw

18. Jewelry
https://www.youtube.com/watch?v=XXjFzDl8bUw

19. Furniture
https://www.youtube.com/watch?v=be5sbDsotlo

20. Vinyl records
https://www.youtube.com/watch?v=sbpXWqX6XY0

Conclusion

Reselling thrifted merchandise is one of the most lucrative and least risky start-up endeavors that you can choose. It is one of the few businesses that have the ideal combination of small investment, efficient sourcing, and online store-friendly and high demand. It is also very rewarding not only because of the profit but also because it satisfies an avid thrifter's passion for thrifting and desire for the thrill of the hunt. Plus, it can act as a safe training ground for future business endeavors.

With the lessons learned from this guide, everything from the types of thrifting stores, the best sellers, the tips on locating and shopping to the videos on assessing quality, the formula for profitability to finally setting up, managing and promoting your business, I hope you are now more than ready and most importantly more confident on your business endeavor.

Resell today and enjoy the profits! Happy thrifting!

Check Out My Other Books

Below you'll find some of my other popular books that are popular on Amazon and Kindle as well. Simply click on the links below to check them out.

http://www.amazon.com/dp/B00S6TOJ5Y

If the links do not work, for whatever reason, you can simply search for these titles on the Amazon website to find them.

53334522R00024

Made in the USA
Middletown, DE
27 November 2017